For the loved ones we've lost, who live on through us.
—E.B.

In memory of the many artist prisoners of Terezin, whose life
and depictions of the Ghetto inspired this book's illustrations greatly.
And for my late grandfather, Captain Simion Rozentsveig, who joined
the Red Army to fight the Nazis when only 16 years old.
—A.R.

Rocky Pond Books
An imprint of Penguin Random House LLC, New York

First published in the United States of America by Rocky Pond Books,
an imprint of Penguin Random House LLC, 2024

Text copyright © 2024 by Elisa Boxer
Illustrations copyright © 2024 by Alianna Rozentsveig

Library of Congress Cataloging-in-Publication Data is available.
Manufactured in China
ISBN 9780593617120
1 3 5 7 9 10 8 6 4 2
TOPL

Design by Jennifer Kelly
Text set in Bohemia LT Std
The art for this book was created digitally using Procreate and Photoshop.

The author gratefully acknowledges the time, insight, and expertise of historian Dr. Anna Hájková of the
University of Warwick, and collections researcher Karen Porter of the National Holocaust Centre and Museum
in England. And heartfelt thanks to Lauri Hornik and Alianna Rozentsveig for bringing this book to life.

The Tree of Life

How a Holocaust Sapling
Inspired the World

written by Elisa Boxer

illustrated by Alianna Rozentsveig

Rocky Pond Books

In a season of sadness, hope came to the children
as a tiny tree, tucked inside a boot.

It was winter, World War Two, and the boot belonged
to a prisoner in a ghetto called Terezin.

There were children in the ghetto too.
The prisoner saw they were scared and
separated from their families.

He also saw a woman secretly teaching the children to read,
write, and celebrate Jewish holidays.

Tu BiShvat was coming —The New Year of the Trees.

The teacher, Irma Lauscher, risked her life when she asked the
prisoner to sneak in a sapling.

The prisoner risked his life when he said yes.

The children were comforted by this living lesson, smuggled in just in time for the holiday. They planted it in a pot.

Then, when the cold ground had thawed,
they dug a hole, put the sapling inside, and
patted down dirt around its base.

The children were thirsty. And they knew the tree must
be thirsty too. So, they lined up with their little cups to share
a few drops a day.

In time, the tree grew taller. Its roots grew stronger. Its branches grew longer.

Prisoners throughout Terezin whispered about this miraculous maple, and how the children managed to make it thrive by sharing what little water they had.

It was known throughout Terezin as *Etz Chaim*: The Tree of Life.

Over time, fewer and fewer children were left
to care for the tree.

With helpless hearts, they watched more and
more of their friends leave . . .

taken away on trains to a place that was even worse.

The children were the future of the Jewish people. And the Nazis wanted a future without Jewish people.

Those who remained never stopped sharing their precious water. Drop after drop, day after day, they kept hope alive.

In time, the tree grew taller.

Its roots grew stronger.

Its branches grew longer.

When the war was over and the prisoners were rescued, the small sapling had grown to five feet—taller than most of the children.

Before walking out of the camp toward freedom, Irma and the children planted a sign in the ground:

"As the branches of this tree, so the branches of our people."

Then, they gathered around it and gave it one final drink.

In time, the tree grew taller. Its roots grew stronger. Its branches grew longer.

As the years went by, people from around the world came to see the ruins of Terezin and say special prayers for all who had died there.

The tree, now sixty feet tall, stood as a silent witness.

And the teacher, Irma, who risked everything to help the children grow this miracle?

She survived the war.

She saw to it that seeds from the tree were planted all over the world, in memory of the children who had kept hope alive.

Sixty years after those children planted and nurtured the sapling, heavy flood waters engulfed the tree.

It stopped growing taller. Its roots became weaker. Its bark fell away.

In 2007, the tree lost its last leaf.

But its 600 sapling descendants
around the world . . .

They grew taller.

Their roots grew stronger.

Their branches grew longer.

In 2021, a miracle came to New York City.

Children cheered and clapped as a fifteen-foot tree was lowered into the ground across from their school.

They'd learned about this tree—about how it was born from a branch of a giant maple, grown in secret by a group of children in the Holocaust.

The students lined up to water it, just like those children nearly eighty years earlier.

Students will continue to care for it, to nourish it, to learn more about its beginnings for generations to come.

In time, this tree will grow taller. Its roots will grow stronger. Its branches will grow longer.

And the world will remember the brave teacher and the children who never gave up nurturing a more hopeful future.

Author's Note

One aspect of the Holocaust I've always found particularly heart wrenching is the fact that countless lives were never allowed to begin. In addition to the lives that were lost, so many generations never even happened; so many family trees never took root.

Ninety percent of Europe's Jewish children were killed in the Holocaust. But despite Hitler's plan to eliminate the Jewish people, descendants of Holocaust survivors are thriving across the world. So too are trees born from that original sapling planted by the children of Terezin.

Seeds and cuttings from the original tree went to places including Israel, England, California, Illinois, and Pennsylvania. Many of them are cared for by congregations and Holocaust museums. And now, there is a tree that will be nurtured by the children of Public School 276 in Battery Park, New York City. The tree, planted outside the Museum of Jewish Heritage, was donated to the museum by Dr. Roger Pomerantz, a Jewish philanthropist who owns a nursery in Pennsylvania, where several descendants of the original tree are flourishing.

Irma Lauscher was the teacher in Terezin, the Czechoslovakian prison camp also known as Theresienstadt. She reportedly asked one of the prisoners to smuggle in a tree sapling to give the children something to nurture and celebrate during their secret lessons about Judaism. These types of lessons were forbidden by the Nazis, as was bringing anything in or out of the camp, so both Irma and the prisoner were putting their lives in danger.

It was a quiet, courageous act of resistance that grows to this day. As a Jewish journalist and author with Eastern European family members on both my mother's and father's sides killed in the Holocaust, I feel an intrinsic drive to illuminate these stories of resistance and triumph.

Terezin was a propaganda camp. The Nazis used it as a façade, to hide the terrible treatment of prisoners. When the Red Cross visited the camp in 1944, they saw well-fed "workers," including children, performing concerts and plays, making art, and engaging in other cultural pursuits. It was all an act. When the Red Cross officials left and reported to the rest of the world that the Nazis were treating their workers very well, the lie was believed and the brutal treatment resumed.

Most of the prisoners, including children, were deported to Auschwitz and killed. Although Terezin was technically a ghetto and not an extermination camp, 34,000 people died there, mostly from disease and starvation.

Irma, the teacher, passed away in 1985. She made arrangements for the tree's seeds and saplings to be distributed and planted around the world in memory of Terezin's children.

During the New York City dedication ceremony for The Children's Tree, Terezin survivor

Fred Terna said: "My feeling of the tree is one word: memory . . . This planting is a form of remembering and that's what this tree is: continuity."

If only those children in Terezin who planted the original tree could have known that something they grew in the darkest of circumstances would be reborn hundreds of times over. If only they could have seen that this symbol of hope they created is now a symbol of survival that will honor the past and nourish the future—for generations to come.

Selected Sources

ARTICLES

"Dedication of The Children's Tree, a Living Artifact from Theresienstadt." Hamodia, December 6, 2021. https://hamodia.com/2021/12/06/dedication-of-the-childrens-tree-a-living-artifact-from-theresienstadt/

Gergely, Julia. "A tree that survived the Holocaust gains a new life in New York City." Israel National News, December 3, 2021. https://www.israelnationalnews.com/news/318027

Glassman, Carl. "Storied Tree, Rooted in the Holocaust, Is Planted to Cheers in BPC." The Tribeca Trib, November 18, 2021. http://www.tribecatrib.com/content/storied-tree-rooted-holocaust-planted-cheers-bpc

Nir, Sarah Maslin. "Planting Hope in Lower Manhattan." The New York Times, December 3, 2021. https://www.nytimes.com/interactive/2021/12/03/nyregion/holocaust-tree-planted-nyc.html

"Holocaust 'Children's Tree' descendant to be planted in NYC." The Jerusalem Post, December 2, 2021. https://www.jpost.com/diaspora/holocaust-childrens-tree-descendant-to-be-planted-in-nyc-687647

Rogelberg, Sasha. "Concentration Camp Sapling Planted at Museum." Jewish Exponent, December 9, 2021. https://www.jewishexponent.com/2021/12/09/concentration-camp-sapling-planted-at-museum/

BOOKS

Hájková, Anna. *The Last Ghetto: An Everyday History of Theresienstadt.* Oxford University Press, 2020.

Harris, Dede. *The Children's Tree of Terezin.* Morton Grove, IL: Legacy Publishing, 2017.

Thomson, Ruth. *Terezin: Voices from the Holocaust.* Candlewick, 2013.

INTERVIEW

Hájková, Anna, in discussion with the author via email, June and July 2022

WEBSITES

Museum of Jewish Heritage. "The Children's Tree: A Living Artifact from Theresienstadt." https://mjhnyc.org/exhibitions/the-childrens-tree-a-living-artifact-from-theresienstadt/

The National Holocaust Centre and Museum. "The Memorial Garden: Terezin Tree." https://www.holocaust.org.uk/discussion-on-links